Ultralight

Ultralight

*The Zen Habits Guide
to Traveling Light and Living Light*

Leo Babauta

WAKING LION PRESS

ISBN 978-1-4341-0474-8

This book is uncopyrighted. The author and publisher release all rights to the work contained herein. Freely use the text as you like.

Cover design by Spyr.

Published by Waking Lion Press, an imprint of the Editorium, LLC.

Waking Lion Press™ and Editorium™ are trademarks of:

The Editorium, LLC
West Jordan, UT 84081-6132
www.editorium.com

The views expressed in this book are the responsibility of the author and do not necessarily represent the position of Waking Lion Press. The reader alone is responsible for the use of any ideas or information provided by this book.

Contents

I	**Ultralight Travel**	**3**
1	Traveling Light Isn't a Competition	5
2	What It's like to Travel with One Bag	7
3	Why We Pack Too Many Clothes, and How to Cut Back	10
4	Clothing System	14
5	Electronics	18
6	Toiletries	21
7	Water and Food	23
8	What You Don't Need	25
9	Don't Pack Your Fears	30
10	What Bag?	33
11	Getting through Airports	36
12	Apartments and Hotels	40

13	Getting around Cities and Where to Go	42
14	Longer Trips	46
15	Flexible Mind, Flexible Travel	49
16	Useful Travel Apps	52
17	Travel Miles and Cards	55
18	My Packing List	58
19	Ultralight Hiking	61
II	**Living Lightly**	**65**
20	What It's like to Live without Too Much Stuff	69
21	Less Clothing	71
22	Books and Papers	73
23	Less Other Stuff	75
24	Electronics and Digital Simplicity	80
25	Dealing with the Urge to Buy	85
26	A Final Word on Living Lightly	89
	About the Author	91

Introduction: Why Travel Light? Freedom from Burden

When Eva and I first started traveling (after being too broke to travel for years), we went to Thailand, then Tokyo, and then London and Paris. We lugged around big duffel bags on those trips, which were checked luggage.

They were loaded up with clothes and toiletries and other things to give us comfort and a feeling of preparedness as we headed out of our comfort zone to new lands.

But we'd get tired from dragging those bags not only on planes but also trains, subways, buses, taxis, and walking along city streets. Travel was fun, but weighed down by these heavy bags.

On the London/Paris trip, we decided we needed to make a change. We barely used most of the things in our big bags. Sure, we were traveling lighter than a lot of people, but we realized we had so much we could cut.

So we started by making a list: what did we *not* use on the last trip? We'd leave those behind next time. What could we do without? We read accounts of other people traveling lightly, both men and women, and decided we were going to cut back.

The result is that our bags got lighter and lighter . . . until they were no longer burdens, but things we barely noticed.

The *freedom* that resulted was so incredible. We felt liberated. We could travel faster, farther, happier. Sure, we gave up a handful of comforts, but in return we got the comfort of being unburdened.

These days we move lightly through our travels as we see people slowed down by big roller luggage, or waiting after a flight for their checked luggage. We get stares from the customs people, who ask, "Is that all you're bringing for two weeks?"

We've traveled for a month with one small backpack each, with no problems. We've gone on multi-week, multi-country trips. We are happier than ever when we travel.

Why travel light? Here's what I've found:

- You don't get as tired.

- You can walk around a city with everything you're carrying and it's no problem.

- Getting through airports is faster and easier.

- You can go through multiple countries and cities without slowing down.

- You learn that you don't need as much.

- You start to become comfortable with less, and able to get by on very little.

- You are liberated from burdens!

I don't judge people with lots of luggage, but I will honestly never go back. I've fallen in love with less, and love traveling the world lightly.

I share this book with you not to brag, not to tell you how to live, but in hopes that you'll find some inspiration from what I've learned, and that you'll love traveling lightly as well.

Part I

ULTRALIGHT TRAVEL

Chapter 1

Traveling Light Isn't a Competition

Once you get into ultralight traveling, it's easy to get into the comparison game: how light is my pack compared to his? Can I get mine smaller so that I'll have some minimalist street cred? I know I've fallen for the temptation, more than once, but I've learned that it's a trap.

This isn't about whose bag is smaller. It's not about being better than anyone else. This is about living life your way, on your terms . . . and finding the freedom to do so by not carrying a huge burden on your back.

So don't get into the trap of comparing your stuff to others' stuff. That's not what this book is about.

It's not about getting your bag to a certain size or weight. It's not about showing off your setup to anyone else. I hesitate to share my setup because I worry about coming across that way, and worry about others trying to compare themselves to me.

But I decided to write this book and share what I do for other reasons:

- In hopes of inspiring people to go lighter and experience the joys of traveling light that I've discovered.

- With the idea of challenging people to rethink their way of doing things, to toss out old ideas and experiment with new ones.

- Because I know others who want to lighten their load but don't know how to get started—and I think that by talking about the nuts and bolts of doing this, it might be useful.

Let's make an agreement: you take away any information and inspiration that you find useful from this book, and don't worry about doing what I do, getting as light (or lighter) than me, comparing yourself to me or anyone else. Deal?

Alright, let's do it then!

Chapter 2

What It's like to Travel with One Bag

I'll walk you through a typical trip, traveling with one light bag.

Planning and Packing

   I start by planning the trip: researching the destination, figuring out dates, booking tickets and an Airbnb apartment, checking out the weather.

   The day before the trip (or often the morning of), I get out my bag and pack. I almost always take the same things, and a lot of those things are stored in one spot in my closet, so packing is as simple as laying everything out, putting them in packing cubes, and tossing them in my bag. It takes 10 minutes. I'll also check in online and get my boarding pass on my phone.

Airport and Plane

I check to make sure I have my passport and other essentials, then hop on a train to the airport. I don't have to check a bag, so long airport lines are skipped.

I have TSA Precheck, so I skip most of the security line and don't have to take off my shoes or take out my laptop . . . so it's about 5–10 minutes through security.

Then I'm at my gate in another 5 minutes. Breezing through the airport means I don't have to get there too early. I still get to the gate about 20 minutes before boarding starts, just because I don't like to rush, but it's a stress-free time for me.

I board the plane, put my small bag under the seat, and start reading or writing. Eventually I get tired of this and watch a movie. Then we arrive and I grab my bag, get off, head through immigration checks, and breeze through customs. I skip the wait for checked baggage at the baggage carousel, so I'm usually out of the airport faster than 95% of other passengers.

The City

I get some foreign currency from an ATM at the airport, then jump on a train to the destination city. At this point I can just start wandering around, get a bite to eat, or find my Airbnb apartment and rest.

I explore the city, usually carrying my bag so I have layers to put on and water if I might need it. Repeat this every day I'm in the city. I might meet up with locals if I have time.

I wash clothes in the sink or shower as needed, usually every 2–3 days, and dry the out in the closet or bathroom, so I always have fresh clothes to wear.

What It's like to Travel with One Bag

If I'm going to multiple cities, I'll pack up my bag and jump on a train to the other city. Or do the airport thing again, but again, it's a simple and easy affair.

Then I go home, unpack a few things, and that's it! Everything is easy, unburdened, light and free.

Of course, not everything is always that ideal, but I'd say for the most part this represents my travel.

Chapter 3

Why We Pack Too Many Clothes, and How to Cut Back

Here's the thing about clothing: everyone brings too many. And there are three main reasons people bring too many clothes:

1. They want to look good. Dress stylish for walking urban streets, look good on the beach, look dressy at restaurants.

2. They plan on going to things that require very specific kinds of clothes. For example, a Michelin starred restaurant in Paris will require a suit with dress shoes.

3. They want to feel prepared. You don't know what situations will come up, where you'll want to go, how you'll feel that day, what the weather will be like . . . so in order to feel prepared, you bring lots of extra clothes.

These are all legitimate reasons, and I'm not going to knock anyone for packing with these reasons (or others).

However, what I've found is that **none of this is necessary.** I've gone on dozens of trips and not needed to pack so much, because I keep my plans simple and learn how to be prepared without bringing too much.

Let's go into these reasons—we'll talk about the first two reasons first, then cover the third reason.

Looking Good and Fancy Occasions

I like to look good as much as the next fellow. However, I have learned to simplify my tastes, and realize that when I go on a trip, pretty much **no one cares how I look**. People are much too focused on how they look, and as long as you don't look like an absolute idiot, they won't even notice. If you look amazing, they probably *still won't notice*. So what's the point?

I keep my color scheme to something really basic (boring blacks, greys, blues) and just focus on looking functionally good. You could choose another color scheme, or wild patterns for all I care, but the main thing is to keep your needs simple.

Another thing I've found is that **no one notices if you wear the same thing every day**. Seriously. It might feel weird to wear the same pants and T-shirt combo every single day, but on the trips I've gone on, either 1) I don't know anyone and rarely see the same people twice, or 2) I hang out with friends (new or old) and they *still* don't notice that I dress the same. Or they do and just accept it because it really doesn't matter. If someone cared so much about how I dressed, they probably wouldn't be a friend of mine, to be honest.

Finally, let's talk about **dressing for certain occasions**. When Eva and I first started traveling, we went to fancy restaurants, and packed extra clothes just for those dinners. Our first trip to Europe (London and Paris), we booked a fancy restaurant every other night, and wore the same nice clothes to all of them . . . but it was still a lot of extra stuff to carry (dress shoes alone take up a lot of space).

We decided after that trip that **we were done.** That was enough for us. We stopped going to fancy restaurants, or only went to ones that were casual enough for us to wear casual clothes. Even fairly nice ones will usually not care if you wear decent but not dressy clothes.

So we have changed our traveling style to fit this kind of packing. Yes, we could go to fancier restaurants or parties or the like, but we're actually **just as happy** going to more casual places. More happy, actually, as it means we have less to carry.

I'm not going to tell you that you shouldn't go wherever you want. I'm only suggesting that you don't *need* to go anywhere fancy in order to have a great trip and be happy.

Being Prepared

We tend to **pack our fears**. That means we pack too much because we think we might need it. We're afraid that we'll be unprepared, so we overpack.

Instead, I've found that all I need is a simple system that prepares for the most likely scenarios—including where we'll be going and what the weather will be like.

First, I think through **where we'll be going.** Are we going to the beach? Hiking in the mountains? Walking city streets? Nice restaurants?

Then I think through what the *minimum* that I need will be. Can I pack shorts that I can swim in and also sleep in and work out in? That means just one pair of shorts!

I also look up **what the weather will be like.** If it's cold, I'll need to bring more layers. Hot means I'll need fewer layers and definitely shorts. I always prepare for rain, because you can't really predict it, and also a light rain jacket is easy to throw in the pack.

The best way to be prepared is to bring layers. Then you can put layers on if it's colder, take them off if it's warmer, and adjust as you go. More layers if it's going to be cold, of course.

I'll get into the details of this system in the next chapter, but for now it's enough to know that you don't need to overpack and bring extras of everything to be prepared. Don't pack your fears!

Chapter 4

Clothing System

Given that we'd like to carry as little extra clothing as possible, it's important to develop a flexible, lightweight clothing system.

Here's what I recommend for such a lightweight system:

1. Take as few extra pieces of clothing as possible.

2. Bring layers, but keep the layers light in most cases (unless you're going into sub-freezing weather, then you'll want some heavier layers).

3. Be willing to wash your clothes by hand every 2–3 days to prevent having to bring extras. You can wash less often if you're willing to wear your clothes a few times before you wash them. For example, I can wear a shirt for at least three days before it needs washing (unless I sweat heavily in it), and pants can go 5–7 days (depending on dirt and sweat levels of whatever activity I'm doing). Underwear is something I only wear once.

I'll usually scope out a destination before deciding on layers—what is the weather going to be like? But in most cases, from spring to fall, I just bring the same things.

Clothing System

Here's my system:

Wear on the plane: Pants (washable, not jeans), underwear (not cotton), shirt (synthetic workout, running or yoga shirt), tennis shoes and running socks. This happens to be the outfit I'll wear almost every day, so I bring clothes that will dry quickly when I wash them.

Layers: Either a synthetic lightweight long sleeve T-shirt to wear over the short sleeve T-shirt, or a fleece hoodie if it's going to be colder. If it's really cold, I'll bring lightweight baselayer bottoms (Patagonia lightweight capilene bottoms) to wear under my pants if needed. I bring a lightweight beanie for head warmth if needed.

Extras: Two extra pairs of underwear and socks. I wash these every day or two, so I don't run out. No extra pants or shirts.

Sleeping or workout: I'll usually bring some running shorts to sleep in, and I can work out in them as well.

Rain: I'll bring a lightweight rain jacket (Patagonia Alpine Houdini or something similarly light and thin). This rain jacket doubles as a windbreaker if it's colder and windy and I need that over my long sleeve shirt or fleece to keep the wind out. No need for rain pants, I can let my pants get wet in the rain. If it's warm enough, I can wear shorts when it's raining, as I don't need rain protection for my legs, and they'll dry off quickly.

That's about it. This setup works in most countries in non-winter weather.

Other than worn clothing (which again, is just pants and a T-shirt and tennis shoes), that's just three extra pieces of clothing, plus two pairs of underwear and socks and light beanie. Super light, works just about everywhere in the world.

Washing Clothes

This system only works if you're willing to:

1. wash clothes every 2–3 days by hand (or in a machine if you rent an Airbnb with a washer); *or*

2. Go for awhile with dirty clothes.

Personally, I can go a couple days without washing as I don't mind wearing clothes a few times before they start to smell. But I don't like to wear smelly clothes. Everyone has their personal preference.

If you're not willing to wash by hand, and you don't like to go too long without washing . . . then you'll have to bring more clothing. But I have to say, you get used to washing by hand. I certainly wasn't at first, but I adjusted quickly, and now it just seems normal. Not difficult at all.

To wash, I just wash in the bathroom sink or in the shower. I'll get the clothing wet, put some soap or shampoo (usually provided in a hotel or Airbnb apartment or hostel) and agitate it a bit, then rinse. Wring it out good, then wrap in a towel and wring out the towel to get out extra moisture. Takes about two minutes, then I hang to dry in the closet or over the bathtub.

It's a simple process. I do recommend synthetic clothing, as it dries very quickly (overnight), especially if you use the towel method I mention above. Plus it dries quickly if you sweat or get caught in the rain. Some people love Merino wool, but as a vegan I haven't tried it and can't recommend it.

Special Circumstances

There are some situations where you need other kinds of clothing. You'll just have to adjust to those each trip.

Some examples:

- **Winter**. If you're going somewhere cold, a puffy insulated jacket and warmer baselayers are a good idea. With a baselayer, a long-sleeve shirt, a fleece or puffy jacket, and a wind she'll, you should be pretty warm. You might need wind pants if it's going to be really cold and windy. And warmer socks and head layers. Do some research beyond this book if you're going into extreme cold.

- **Very hot places**. In tropical weather, you're unlikely to need the base layers and warmer clothing. Shorts, T-shirts, and flip flops are better bets, along with bug and sun protection if needed. In desert climates, you'll want to do a little more research, as my clothing system isn't designed for extremes like that.

- **Special sports**. Obviously if you're going skiing, trekking into the mountains, running an ultramarathon, sailing or doing some other kind of special activity, you'll need to figure out what you need. But the same ideas can apply—don't take the maximum you *might* need, but the minimum you're likely to need.

Again, do some research, and figure out what your needs are. Then pack the minimum layers necessary.

Chapter 5

Electronics

I'm a minimalist (kind of) when it comes to electronics, but I'm not a Luddite. I don't really go on "vacations"—my trips are a combo of working/vacation trips, so I enjoy a destination but I also work every day. So I need things like a phone and a laptop.

That said, I think we can easily overdo it. We don't need a thousand gadgets and cords, just a handful.

Here's what I bring:

1. **Phone and cord**. I use an iPhone 6s at the moment, with T-Mobile family plan that includes free international data in most countries. Plus the power cord.

2. **Small extra battery**. I rarely need an extra battery, as I charge my phone every night and pretty much never run out during the day. But when I do, it's nice to have half a charge to get me home. So I pack a Mophie power reserve (1,300 mAh), which just weighs 1.5 oz and can be charged with my iPhone cord.

3. **Laptop and cord**. I use the latest MacBook, which is just 2 lbs. (less than 1kg). It's not a powerhouse, but

I can do everything I need for work on this, and it's pretty lightweight.

4. **Lightweight power adapter**. I bring the Kikkerland universal travel adapter everywhere. It's small, adapts to pretty much every power outlet system I've ever seen, weighs very little.

That's all I need for any trip.

What I Don't Bring

Now, I realize my needs are different than yours . . . but here's what I don't bring anymore:

- **Camera**: I actually have a fairly nice DSLR, and it takes amazing photos. But it's heavy, and I actually dislike carrying it around. Yes there are lightweight digital cameras, but they're not that much better than my phone's camera. Of course, I'm not a professional photographer, but for the rest of us, I'd say a phone is enough. And this means you don't need extra batteries for the camera, a battery charger, a camera case, etc.

- **Big reserve battery**: Some people bring 10K mAh batteries, but unless you're going to be off the grid for 5–6 days, I've found those unnecessary. Let's say you're going to be off the grid for 3 days . . . you can put your phone on airplane mode, and still take pics and connect to the Internet every once in awhile to check on things. As long as you're not using the phone all day, your battery can last for a few days.

- **Kindle**. I actually have a Kindle, and love it. But I can read just as well on my phone.

- **Tablet**: It's funny, because as I write this, I'm writing on an iPad mini with a lightweight keyboard. It all weighs in at about a pound, half of what my laptop weighs. It's not bad, but I much prefer my laptop for getting work done. Tablets are nice for watching movies, but I can do that on my laptop as well.

- **Portable wifi router**. These are cool, but I've found the T-mobile international data plan enough for me. So I skip this.

The ideas is to get away from single-purpose devices like the Kindle and camera, and see what you can do with the 1–2 multi-purpose devices you bring.

Chapter 6

Toiletries

I'm (fairly) minimalist when it comes to toiletries as well. I used to bring a lot more, but now I've found I don't need very much.

Here's what I bring:

- Travel toothbrush
- Travel toothpaste
- Travel deodorant
- Travel electric clippers (for shaving my head)
- Dental floss
- Ibuprofen (about 6 pills, just in case)
- Leuko tape (small roll, for blister prevention)
- Nail clippers
- Ear plugs
- Eye mask
- Razor (I use soap to shave my face with this razor)

This all fits in a very small toiletry bag. I've found this suits my needs very well.

I realize that others have different needs. Some of you have hair, so you need a comb and hair product perhaps. Women have additional needs, from makeup to feminine hygiene products. I'm not going to tell you what to bring. The idea is to see how little you can get by with.

Chapter 7

Water and Food

I don't normally take a lot of water and food with me, but I thought I'd address this topic as these are essential parts of travel. They don't require a ton of packing or planning, however.

Water

You usually can't bring water through airport security, but it's good to have water on a plane and when you move around your destination. So I like to bring either a collapsible water bottle (by Vapur or Playtpus, for example) or just an empty plastic water bottle. These are lighter than the aluminum reusable bottles you'll see a lot of people using, which are great but bulky and heavy.

So bring an empty collapsible water bottle, and fill up at the airport after security so you'll have water on the plane. You can also carry a bit of water with you as you walk around, and refill as needed.

Some destinations don't have drinkable water. Look it up before you go, because you don't want to get sick—that doesn't make for a great trip. At these destinations, just buy bottled water, and drink and brush your teeth with that. Simple, easy.

Food

As a vegan, it can be slightly more difficult to find eating choices in airports and places that are filled with fast food. I mean, I can always find fruit, salad, French fries, things like that . . . but options are more limited sometimes. So I used to often pack a few vegan energy bars, but honestly I rarely need them so I've stopped packing them.

I use the Happy Cow app for vegan traveling, and also will look up good vegan restaurants before I travel and mark them with a star on Google Maps. That way I have an app with great eating options wherever I go, and a map with some places to check out. You can do this if you're not vegan but particular about food—healthy options, gluten-free options if you have celiacs disease, or maybe you're just a foodie who wants good places to check out.

What this means is that I often don't eat everything that other travelers eat. There are dozens of pastry shops, fast food places, stands with fried meats . . . and I'm OK with missing out on these. Honestly, the food I eat is so delicious that I don't mind walking an extra half mile to find them, and I don't mind missing out on what other people find delicious. I don't feel I'm missing out at all!

That said, if I'm worried about there being vegan options, I address this fear with some research. Google and Happy Cow are my friends. What can I eat? What can I find in food markets, street vendors, grocery stores? I look this all up ahead of time. And if I can, I'll ask locals.

In the end, eating doesn't have to involve a lot of work or stress. Be less picky, do a bit of research, and enjoy yourself.

Chapter 8

What You Don't Need

If you noticed the lists in the previous chapters, they're all pretty minimal. Sure, some people could travel with even less, but the idea is to figure out what the essentials are, and leave behind the rest. This might take some experimentation.

OK, so here's a list of things I have found to *not* be essential. It's totally fine to take some of them as luxury, non-essential comfort items . . . but you probably don't want to take too many of them!

Here's the list:

- Nice clothes - suits, fancy dresses, things you'd wear to a high-end restaurant or on the runway. Go for simplicity and comfort!

- Nice shoes - If you don't bring the nice clothes, you don't need the nice shoes. Go casual, and make sure they're comfortable for walking all day around a city.

- Extra clothes - see the clothing system I described, and adapt it for your needs . . . but you don't need an outfit for every day you're going to travel. This takes up the bulk of most people's big suitcases, so if you can reduce the extra clothing to a minimum, your luggage can be drastically reduced, down to a small backpack!

- Extra shoes - just bring the one pair. Seriously, I've never needed more than one pair, though I've often considered bringing more than one pair. I like either running shoes or Converse-style lowtops.

- Cotton clothes, jeans - everyone loves jeans! And cotton! But they're heavy, they aren't easy to wash, they take forever to dry, they're uncomfortable and cold when they're wet, and they can chafe if they're wet and you're walking around in them all day. Wear synthetics!

- Jacket - these are bulky and not necessary for most places, even if it's fairly cold. A wind/rain shell over fleece and base layer or T-shirt is good enough for most places. Add an extra layer if it's colder.

- Hair straightener, dryer, curling iron - OK, I'm biased because I have a shaved head (OK, bald) . . . but even my wife with her long lovely hair has dropped these items from her pack. She just combs her hair now, and some places have hair dryers but often she'll just let it dry naturally. Simple!

- Hair product - Eva gave up using hair products, just goes au natural and everything is fine. And I can confirm she looks good.

- Lots of makeup - Eva brings a little makeup, but she's dropped most of her makeup kit from her travel pack. I think she takes like three little things. Yes, some women will feel they need a lot more, but I challenge you to go minimal and see if you can function without it.

What You Don't Need 27

- Lots of toiletries - I've never used very much in this department, but Eva used to be a lot less of a minimalist here. She's stripped this down to a small pouch that does the trick.

- Wipes - baby wipes, disinfectant wipes. Drop them.

- First aid kit - I've never needed this. A few ibuprofen pills should do the trick.

- Paper books - trust me, I love paper books as much as anyone. I used to always have at least one paper book on every trip, and I still end up buying a book on some trips if I happen upon an amazing independent bookshop, just because I can't resist, plus I want to support these small booksellers. But honestly, books are heavy, and you can load a thousand on your phone with zero extra weight.

- Notebooks - for years I would bring along a Moleskine notebook, hoping to journal or write or sketch. Barely ever happened, found I don't need this. Just write in my phone or laptop.

- Travel pillow - these are nice, and bring one if you want, but most of these are bulky (the non-inflatable ones) and the inflatable ones aren't that comfortable. I make do without.

- Towel - if you're a big fan of HItchhiker's Guide to the Galaxy, like I am, you'll gasp at the suggestion that you don't need a towel. But you almost never do. Hotels and Airbnb apartments all have them, and you can buy locally if you ever need one.

- Soap - if you have sensitive skin, you might want to bring your special soap, but you can buy most kinds of soap at your destination, probably. I've barely ever needed to buy soap where I go because it's usually provided wherever I'm staying.

- MP3 player - use your phone.

- Bluetooth speaker - you're not a DJ. Bring earphones!

- DSLR camera and assorted lenses and gear - if you're serious about photography, sure, bring a small DSLR camera. But most of us just want some nice travel photos we can share or document our trip with, and your camera phone works just fine for that.

- GoPro - most people aren't adventure travelers, just use your camera phone.

- Flashlight - use your phone, but you probably won't need it.

- Power converter - an adapter is necessary in most foreign countries, but you don't need a converter, I've found.

- Electric toothbrush - I use one of these at home. When I travel, I go old school.

- Sunglasses - some people find these indispensable. And I'm sure if you're going into the snow, you need them. Otherwise, I think they're non-essential.

- Jewelry - you're not traveling to win a fashion show. Unless you're a model, traveling to a fashion show. Then, you know, do what you need to do.

- Guidebooks - I used to always buy a guidebook for whatever destination I'm going to, but it's bulky and most of it isn't needed. Instead, now I do research online and save the key info to a doc that I create that's accessible on my phone.

- A daypack—some people bring a bigger backpack (55L for example) and then a daypack for walking around. Just bring the daypack!

- Anything you can buy if you need to - if you *might* need it but you can buy it where you're going, just leave it behind. You probably won't need it, and you can always find it if you do.

This list isn't complete (there are *lots* of other things you don't need), nor is it a judgment on anyone who brings these things. I only want to bring these up so you'll give them a second thought, perhaps drop some of them if you agree you don't need them.

However, you don't always need to bring the bare minimum. If you want to bring along non-essentials because they'll make your trip better, then that's totally fine. I do it sometimes too, especially if it's not too much weight or bulk. As they say in hiking, "Hike your own hike."

Chapter 9

Don't Pack Your Fears

In the last chapter, we talked about things you probably don't need to bring. I'm guessing many of you will want to bring some of those items, and other non-necessities . . . not out of a desire for comfort, but because of a **fear that you might need them**.

I learned from ultralight backpacking that people **pack their fears**. We all do, myself included.

What does this mean? We bring along more than we need because of our fears. We are worried about unexpected conditions:

- What if there's a storm?
- What if I have to go to a nightclub?
- What if I get blisters, or an injury?
- What if I get stuck somewhere with not enough TV shows to watch?
- What if I get a tear in my clothes?
- What if I get mugged?
- What if it gets really cold? Snows?

And so on. All of these "what ifs" represent fears of the unknown, uncertainty. And our way of dealing with that uncertainty and fear is to try to feel prepared, by packing more.

I'm here to tell you that you don't need to pack more. That with some research, you can figure out whether it is likely to snow. That you can figure out how to deal with a robbery, blister, injury, tear in your clothing . . . without needing to pack a lot of extra things.

A lot of these fears lessen when you get more experience. What you gain is a trust that you'll be able to handle things when they come up, and the knowledge that usually, none of these fears every actually come true. A trust that things will work out just fine.

This comes with experience, because at first, you have no idea what will happen, and the fears can be overwhelming. I'm suggesting that you experiment with dropping your extra stuff immediately, without needing all the experience, and see if you can get by without it. See if you can handle your fears without needing to pack for them. Trust that things will work out, despite the fears.

The fears aren't true, and you are more capable than you might realize. For every fear, find out how to deal with it without packing for it—how can you deal with the most common problems on a trip without packing for them?

For example, wearing good running shoes or shoes meant for walking can cut way down on blisters, along with wearing good synthetic running socks. You can pack a little leukotape (maybe a meter or so, rolled up on itself) to cover any hotspots that develop. For a tenth of an ounce, you've prevented blisters! Or buy the tape at your destination, only if needed.

Same for any other kind of injury—every place, unless you're away from civilization, has pharmacies, so you can buy whatever you need if you get hurt. And most injuries never ever happen anyway.

If you're having fears and not wanting to give up things in your pack because of those fears . . . try this:

- Write down your fear
- Write down the thing you want to pack
- Research how likely the fear is to happen
- Research if there are ways to deal with the likely ones without packing anything
- Try going without it and see what happens

If you do pack your fears, make a note after every trip about whether the fear came true or not, and what you needed and didn't need. Eventually you'll be able to let them go.

Chapter 10

What Bag?

Most people put a lot of thought into what bag(s) to bring on a trip, because a bag can be seen as part of your identity. I'll be honest, I am no exception to this, even if I don't think we should identify with our stuff. I'm human!

One bag. I think you should bring one bag. Not a suitcase and a carry on, just a carry on. And just one carry on. It makes everything easier, and forces you to choose instead of allowing you to bring a thousand "just in case" items. One bag is minimal, light, easy, convenient, and forces choices.

A backpack. I always travel with a backpack, because it's the easiest thing to walk around a city with. A backpack with a light load—less than 15 lbs. (6.8kg), preferably less than 10 lbs.(4.5kg)—is super easy to carry around. A roller bag, on the other hand, seems easy if your load is heavier, but it makes going up and down escalators, through security, through metro stations and on subways and taxis, all through a city on sidewalks and crosswalks, so much harder. Get a good backpack, don't overload it, and you're golden.

Less than 20 liters (or so). This will be controversial, because everyone has different needs. Most people, traveling with one bag, will want something larger than 30 or 40 liters in volume. But I've found, unless you have certain specific needs (like you're a professional photographer or athlete), the average traveler can get by with less than 20 liters. Even if you're traveling for a month or two. Follow the recommendations of this book and you can do it. I can get by with less than 15 liters (even less than 10 liters most times), but my bag is around 20 liters because it's the best bag I know of for traveling (Minaal Daily) so I go around with it almost half empty. Most people can do less than 20 liters if they try.

Other than those recommendations, there are lots of good choices! Here are just a handful:

1. **Minaal** (minaal.com). I think of these guys, who are friends of mine, as the gold standard of travel bag. Yes, it's a little more expensive, but if you travel a lot, it's what you're going to live in. So you want quality, and you want a lot of smart features. They're usual carry on is big, like 34 liters (they hate volume measurements for bags), but they have a day pack called the Minaal Daily that's just about perfect. I cut out some of the extra pockets and features to make it even lighter, but this is what I travel with all the time now, through more than 20 cities so far.

2. **Tom Binh**. I've actually never owned one of these but a lot of travelers swear by these bags. They look well made and lightweight, a good combo. I'd look at the Synapse 19 if I were going to get one of their packs.

3. **Osprey**. A lot of people love this brand for backpacks. I think they're perfectly fine, but most of their travel packs are meant for the average traveler, which means 40L or more. I'd look at their Talon 22 or Escapist 18 for something smaller.

There are dozens and dozens of other good options out there. The actual bag doesn't matter as much as what you put in it, and what you get out of it.

Chapter 11

Getting through Airports

The good news is that traveling light makes the hassle of getting through airports nearly stress free. Seriously, along with a couple other tips, traveling through airports no longer stresses me out, and is actually enjoyable.

Here's what I do to travel lightly through airports:

1. **No checked bag**. As I've made abundantly clear, I travel with just a lightweight backpack. No checked bags, only one carry on. So when I go to the airport, I just walk to security and skip the airline counter check-in.

2. **Check in online, boarding pass on phone**. I think most people do this (checking in online) these days, but combined with no checked bags, this means you cut down on what you have to do when you get to the airport, and the amount of time it takes. After I check in online, I do my best to get a mobile boarding pass, so I don't need to print anything. If I can't get it on my phone (so airlines are behind the times), I print it at an airline kiosk at the airport, takes about 2 minutes.

3. **Get Global Entry/TSA Precheck**. For U. S. citizens only, but if you are this is worth it—apply for Global

Entry and you get enrolled in the TSA Precheck program automatically. It's a bit of a hassle (lengthy online application, then get an appointment for a short interview at the airport) and it costs like $100. But some (good) travel credit cards will reimburse this fee (see travel miles chapter) and it's good for 5 years, which is just $20 or so per year, totally worth it if you take more than one or two trips a year. Why is it worth it? Because you skip long lines at (most) TSA security checkpoints, and don't have to take off your shoes or belt, go through the porno scanner, nor take out your laptop. Really cuts down on the hassle. And if you travel to another country, when you return to the U.S., you skip the lines and it takes like 30 seconds to get through immigration.

4. **Streamline the security check-in process**. Whether you have TSA Precheck or not, there are a few things you can do to make the security checkpoints easier. I don't wear a belt—pants that fit well work for me. I take everything out of my pockets (including phone and passport) and throw it in a pocket in my backpack, while I'm standing in line, so that when I get to the screening conveyor belt, I just put my bag on the conveyor belt and walk through the metal detector. That simple! Most other people are fumbling with a million things when they get to the conveyor belt, which just slows everything down.

5. **Get there slightly early**. If you do all of the above points, by the time you arrive at the airport, you have about 10–15 minutes before you're at your gate. And since you don't need to arrive at your gate until 15 minutes before departure (you don't have to board when they *start* the boarding process!), you really only need to get to the airport like 30 minutes before departure time. *However* . . . lines can be unpredictable. So I

like to get to the airport about 80–90 minutes before departure time, which means I have about an hour or more at the gate. That's not a problem, because I just get out my laptop and do some work while I top off my phone battery at an available outlet. This removes all stress, getting there a bit early. I don't recommend 2 hours early, that's way too much cushion if you've streamlined like I have.

Honestly, airports aren't that bad, even if you don't streamline as much as I do. I just like to make it even easier.

Arriving at a Destination Airport

After your plane lands, you need to get through the airport and to your apartment or hotel. This part is pretty stress free too.

Here's what I do:

1. **Immigration.** In other countries, there's nothing that can be done about this. Just fill out any forms you can on the plane, have your passport ready, get in line. Returning to the U.S., I skip the lines because of Global Entry.

2. **Skip the baggage claim.** I breeze past the people waiting for their luggage at baggage claim, as I only have the one light backpack. I often go through customs and get the question, "This is all you're carrying for two weeks?" and I answer with a smile, "Yep, I travel light!"

3. **Get some cash.** In a foreign country, the best way to get the local currency is at an ATM. I just hit one up at the airport.

4. **Transport**. I will always take a train from the airport if one is available. I look up how to catch the train from the airport before I depart from my airport of origin, including how to get to my hotel or Airbnb apartment from the train station.

Pretty simple, nothing mind-blowing there, but that's what I do.

Chapter 12

Apartments and Hotels

Sometimes, as a treat, I book a luxury hotel for Eva and I so that it can feel like a wonderful getaway trip. While luxury hotels are really nice, I've been finding more and more that I prefer to stay in an apartment. So I book through Airbnb (or similar service).

An apartment in a destination city makes everything easy, even if it's a small one. For example, in Tokyo, I book tiny apartments near Shibuya station (my favorite central neighborhood in the city) and it's much cheaper than getting a hotel. If I want to save even more, I can book further away from the center, but it saves so much time to be right in the center that I always spend an extra $20/night for the convenience.

Even a tiny apartment in Tokyo gets me:

- A bathroom (which a shared hostel doesn't do)

- My own place (which shared hostel or couchsurfing don't do)

- A kitchen (which a hotel doesn't do)

- Wifi (which some hotels charge extra for)

Apartments and Hotels 41

- Sometimes a washer and dryer (which almost nothing else gets you)
- Living room space for work, lounging, etc. (which almost nothing else gets you)

It's cheaper than a hotel, and I'm getting more! It's more expensive than couchsurfing or hostels (usually), but I find the convenience to be worth it for me. If you're on a super tight budget, I recommend couchsurfing (free).

Some people who normally get a hotel don't like Airbnb because it seems inconvenient. You have to meet someone to check in! Actually, most hosts these days have a simple way to check in like a lockbox or mailbox with a combination lock to get the keys, so you never need to see anyone if you don't want to. That only applies if you're getting a full apartment rather than sharing a room or getting a private room within a shared apartment, but I pretty much always get a full apartment. If you're on a budget, sharing is cheaper.

Some people like a hotel housekeeper to clean up their room every morning, and like room service. That's fine, but I find it wasteful as I don't need my room cleaned every day, my sheets changed, etc. And room service is super expensive, so I like to buy stuff at a grocery store if I'm going to eat in, or get out and explore the city's restaurants.

Travel however you like, I'm not judging. This style works for me.

Chapter 13

Getting around Cities and Where to Go

Once you're in your destination city and settled into your apartment, getting around is the fun part.

I can walk all day with my full travel kit, but if I have an apartment or hotel, I'll usually unpack when I get there and just carry a few essentials in my backpack:

- Rain jacket
- Sweater/extra top layer if it might be cold
- Beanie
- Backup battery
- Water
- Any of Eva's stuff if she wants me to carry it
- I can also buy some snacks at a grocery store to carry around if I want

If I don't think it'll rain, I'll just throw the little backup battery in my pocket and go without a backpack. Either way is super light and easy.

Getting around Cities and Where to Go

Transportation

I almost always use one of these:

- **Walking**. This is my favorite. I walk everywhere I can. It's the best way to see a city, and again, if I'm traveling light, it's easy and fun.

- **Public transport**. I almost always do a little research on the local transport system, and often will get a refillable card or pass to get around to different neighborhoods. Usually I'll ride the metro to a different neighborhood and then walk all day in that area, then ride the metro back to my apartment. It's easy and fun and you feel like a local, plus you see locals riding so you learn a bit about them.

- **Uber or cabs**. I really like Uber's service, if a city has them and it would save me 30 minutes or more from public transport, I'll use Uber. Or a cab if they don't. The cost can add up, though, so I try to do the other two above.

- **Bikes**. Some cities have a public bike sharing program. Or you can rent a bike. To be honest, I barely use this, but I think it's a great option. I prefer walking to explore a city, though.

- What I really avoid:

- **Tour buses**. I find that they're too touristy, and they're no fun, and they keep you on the path that crowds and crowds of other tourists are on. Get off that path! Get into local neighborhoods! More on that below, but generally I avoid tour buses like the plague.

- **Tour groups**. I don't like being led, I like exploring on my own. That said, some walking tours can be fantastic if you have a great local guide. I recommend skipping these, looking stuff up and exploring on your own, or even better, finding a local to hang out with.

- **Cabs/Uber everywhere**. I said above that I like Uber, but some people take them everywhere. I don't judge them, but I don't find that to be a good way to get to know a place. Instead, walk! Or ride public transit if you need to go further distances. Uber is to be used as a backup.

Where to Go

I really don't like tourist areas. They are massively crowded and expensive, and don't give you the flavor of a place at all. I'm talking about places like Fisherman's Wharf in San Francisco—skip this and find areas not targeted at tourists!

That said, there are some historic places, like the Coliseum in Rome, that I would not skip even if every tourist goes there, just because they are so important that you have to go at least once. I don't think an entire trip should be spent on places like this, though.

What's a better way? Well, here's what I like:

- **Explore neighborhoods**. I will usually research some of the best neighborhoods in a new city before we leave, then mark some of the coolest spots on Google Maps. Then we just walk and explore, without an itinerary, letting ourselves get lost and find stuff by accident, mostly. Sometimes we'll head in the direction of something on my map, but let ourselves meander along the way.

- **Talk to locals**. If I can meet up with a local, that's absolutely the best thing. They might want to show me a couple of their favorite spots, but even if they don't, I ask them where to go. Best parks? Restaurants? Museums? Hidden spots no one knows about? Places locals like to hang out on a weekend? Rooftop spots? If I can't meet up with a local, I'll read blogs by locals or email someone who might know.

- **Find gems from people who know.** If I want to find the best vegan restaurants, I'll use Happy Cow, but even better, I'll ask vegans in that city. If I want to find the best walks, I'll ask locals. I ask museum experts or history experts or art experts where to go for those kinds of places, if I can. Or read their blogs.

- **Look for history and literature**. I love learning about the history of a place, so I'll look up guides and blogs that help me explore a city's history on foot. And if I can find some places with literary history, that's my favorite!

In the end, you don't need all the recommendations and guide books in the world. A few are enough to get you started, but in general, the best way to explore is just by discovery. Get out and walk, and see what you can find!

Chapter 14

Longer Trips

Traveling light for a few days or even a week is great, but what if you're traveling longer? For a few weeks, or a month? What about a couple months, a year, indefinitely?

The length of the trip does change things, but I think the ideas are pretty much the same. And it doesn't change things as much as many people might think.

So I have to admit, I've only traveled with a lightweight kit like I describe for a month or so, definitely not longer than 5–6 weeks. But traveling for a month and using the same stuff, without any problems, makes me think that I could do it for much longer. At least a few months.

What would change if the trip were for 6 months, a year, or indefinite?

Here's what I think might be different:

- **Cold weather.** If I were in a place or several places that had snowy winters, I'd probably need some warmer clothes. I'd still go with the layers, though: baselayers, mid layers, outer shell for wind/rain/wetness protection. I don't think you'd need that many more clothes, but I'd have to think about head and feet and hand protection from the cold.

- **Wider range of weather and needs**. If you're traveling around the world, to more places and for a longer time, that might mean your conditions are going to vary from hot and humid tropical to desert climate to cold weather. And you might go from jungle to city to mountains. A wider range of conditions requires a little more stuff, but I would keep the extra stuff to light layers that can be use modularly—take some off if it's hot, add some more if it's cold. I'd go for things that could provide wind, rain, sun, and snow protection at once.

- **Toiletries**. My travel toiletries can last for a few weeks, but they're so small that I'd need to replace them while traveling. That's pretty easy to do, just buy them as you travel. In fact, you could do the same for any clothes, shoes, electronics—anything you need, you could replace or add to as you travel, even prescription stuff for the most part.

- **Longer-term apartments**. I wouldn't rent by the day, I'd rent by the month, if I were to travel indefinitely. I'd probably get an Airbnb at my destination for a week while I look for a longer-term place. This would allow me to buy a few extra comfort things if I wanted them, including a few cooking pans/utensils/dishes, though I wouldn't get a lot of stuff just in case I had to move.

- **Working out**. I'd find a gym, or do bodyweight stuff with running and hiking. I *love* to hike. Or maybe find a new hobby like rock climbing.

I can't think of anything else I'd need. Your needs will be different, of course, but I think it would be worthwhile to think about what you'd really need vs. what you think you *might* need, even if you travel for longer.

Even when I'm at home, I don't have too many more things than I have when I travel, other than workout stuff and kitchen stuff. I have some extra clothes, to be sure, and maybe a couple extra toiletry things. Some extra books, a desktop computer and printer, scanner and router for working. If I had to, I could do without pretty much all of these things.

Chapter 15

Flexible Mind, Flexible Travel

This book isn't about getting to the most minimalist setup. It's not about the perfect travel setup, getting everything just right so that you feel prepared and wipe out uncertainty.

This book is really about flexibility, both in your setup and in your mindset.

So I'd like to talk briefly about flexibility, and how and why to develop a flexible mindset as you travel.

Why Flexibility

When you have inflexibility, it causes problems.
For example:

- If you have set expectations of a trip, and things go differently, you'll be disappointed.

- If you are fixed on the plans you made, and things get changed up, you'll be stressed out.

- If you want an itinerary to go exactly as you planned, you'll stress about making things go perfectly.

- If you hope that someone will behave a certain way during your trip, and they behave differently, you'll be disappointed.
- If you're hoping for a certain kind of hospitality, or weather, or scenery from your trip, and you don't get it, you might be frustrated or disappointed.

You get the idea. These are fairly obvious, but most people don't realize how many of their difficulties are caused by fixed ideas and expectations. And how many can be solved by flexibility.

Flexibility, in contrast, helps you to let go of what you were hoping for or what you want, and instead go with the flow. You are able to adjust to changes more easily, are less frustrated, are more at peace during your trip (and at other times).

How to Create a Flexible Mindset

The first thing to notice is when you're getting stressed in some way (disappointment, frustration, anxiety, anger, stress). Notice that you're feeling the stress, see it as a flag that something is going on.

See the inflexibility, see that you're holding on, that you want things a certain way. See how it's causing you stress.

Sit with the stress for a minute, just facing it instead of lashing out, running away, seeking to gain control. Just sit and notice it, see how it feels, which takes courage.

And then let go. Just relax the inflexibility, relax into the moment, accept that things are not the way you wanted, accept how they are, and adjust. Go with the flow. Smile, breathe, see the beauty in front of you.

Appreciate what you have, instead of focusing on the way things aren't. Find gratitude.

If you can practice this regularly, you can develop flexibility, the ability to let go, the ability to mindfully pause and relax and find gratitude.

This is flexibility, and it makes traveling light much more peaceful and wonderful.

Chapter 16

Useful Travel Apps

I'm going to be honest, I haven't tried every single travel app, nor have I used Android in years, so this is going to be an incomplete list, and you should probably do your own research.

That said, I have a slew of apps I use regularly when I travel, ones that I find very useful.

Here they are:

1. **Tripit**. I love this app so much I pay for the pro version. It's pretty simple: when you get an airline or hotel or car rental confirmation email, you just forward the email to Tripit. It gets added automatically to a trip itinerary, without you needing to create one. Now you have all of your itinerary info in one place, to check whenever you travel. The pro version has some nice features like update notifications if your flight gets delayed or moved to a new gate, and reminders to check in 24 hours before, with a check-in link.

2. **Google Maps**. This one is obvious, but I use it all the time to walk around and get to know a city. It gives me transit directions, walking directions, biking directions. I can star the places and restaurants I want to check

Useful Travel Apps

out. Download the city map you plan to use for offline use before you leave, in case you won't have data.

3. **Google Flights**. At the risk of sounding too Google-centric (guilty), I use Google Flights to search for the best flight options. It only got good recently, but now it's my favorite flight search tool, and it's pretty uncluttered compared to others.

4. **T-Mobile**. This isn't an app, but a cell phone plan, for U. S. readers of course. If you're willing to switch, get one of their data plans that includes *unlimited international data* in most countries. It was a game-changer for me. Yes, it's just 2G speeds, but it's so convenient to just have unlimited data and not worry about the cost, that I don't mind slower speeds.

5. **Airbnb**. I mentioned how much I use these guys. Their app is also beautiful and easy to use. Great for messaging your host if you have questions, or searching for a new place in your next city while traveling.

6. **Uber**. I also mentioned that I use these guys regularly. Yes, Lyft is just as good. I'm not a fan of everything Uber does. But they work in more cities than anyone else, so I use them.

7. **Kayak**. I use this app not only for flight searches, but more for hotel searches in a pinch. If I'm suddenly in a city without a place to stay, I'll look on here for a cheap, quick hotel room. It's easy to use.

8. **Happy Cow**. For vegans and vegetarians, this is *the* app to use when you travel and want lots of food options.

9. **Whatsapp**. The messaging app that's used internationally, I find this a good way to stay in touch with friends all over the world, but also to create a group if I'm

traveling with several people, so we can stay in touch while on a trip. So useful. Plus no texting fees, and you can make free phone calls.

10. **Airline apps and Apple Wallet**. I usually have a few airline apps downloaded, mostly to check in for my flights and get a mobile boarding pass. Once I have the boarding pass, I add it to Apple Wallet because it's an easy place to keep all my boarding passes.

11. **Google Translate**. Really helps when you don't speak the language. But learn at least a handful of phrases, you lazy Americans! ;)

12. **Yelp**. Not really useful in many countries outside of the U.S., but it's growing. And in the U.S., it's a great way to find places you're looking for, from restaurants to coffee shops to bookstores and more, read reviews, check out photos, get the opening hours and address, and more.

13. **Convert**. Just a free app to convert currency. Also converts units of measurement, which can be handy, but the currency conversion is the most useful.

14. **Dark Sky**. This is actually just my daily weather app (yes, it's a paid app but worth it). But it's great for checking out the forecast for my destinations before I go, not only for rain/sun/snow and temperature, but also wind, UV index, chances of precipitation and more, all by the hour. Useful when you're at a place and deciding what to wear today.

OK, those are my favorites, and I use most of them on every trip. Hope you find them useful!

Chapter 17

Travel Miles and Cards

I'm not a rich guy. I'm not the poorest, but I don't live a jet set lifestyle where I can fly first class around the globe and live it up. I have a budget, but I still travel.

How? Using airline award miles (and saving up of course).

I'm also not the world's foremost expert on travel miles. For that, you might try thepointsguy.com. Especially his "Hot Deals" page . . . it outlines the best cards to get right now.

But here's what I've been doing, which isn't as much as a lot of people do, but it's enough for me:

1. **Sign up for credit cards with bonus miles.** You can get bonus miles of 40K, 50K, even 100K sometimes. That's one or two trips to Europe! That usually requires you to spend a certain amount within a few months . . . see the next item.

2. **Put spending on your most recent cards.** I have one main card for business, one for personal expenses . . . and I put pretty much all my spending on these two cards. Travel expenses, groceries, gas, rent, utilities, cell phone, even paying vendors for my business. That means that I not only make the bonus miles for the first few months of spending on a new card . . . but every

dollar I spend is earning me points. That means each year, I'm earning tens of thousands (if not hundreds of thousands) of award miles.

3. **Learn how to transfer.** When I first started, I didn't understand how all the award systems worked. But now I know the broad strokes . . . like that I can transfer among the two most common airline award alliances, or use separate point systems like Chase points or Starwood points and then transfer them to airline award systems when needed. So I usually have like 5–7 different pools of award points, and just transfer as needed.

4. **Pay off cards immediately.** I used to be **very** anti-credit cards, because using them badly got me into a lot of debt trouble, and it took years to get out of it. But now I've learned to not spend more than I have, and pay off my cards immediately. I don't spend just because I have the cards, I have a spending plan but just pay for everything using the cards. And then pay off the card before it's due, or at the very least auto-pay it on its due date. This way I never have to pay interest, which is the worst use of your money.

5. **Every now and then, apply for new cards.** The bonus miles you get to sign up are the best. So when I see a hot new deal with 50K or 100K bonus miles, I grab it. That might mean letting go of some old cards, but I keep my oldest ones just to keep my credit score high.

Oh, building good credit matters a lot. I'm approved because I have good credit. If you don't have good credit, do some research and start building it.

Yes, there are lots of other ways to get miles, and lots of tricks. I don't find it worth my time to research all of these.

I have friends who do mileage runs, who learn all the ways to get into airline lounges at airports . . . those don't matter to me at all. I'm perfectly happy sitting in a regular airport seat and doing my work, and I'm not going to spend time doing mileage runs.

I also don't worry about getting to certain tiers in airline award systems (like platinum, gold, silver, etc.). It would be cool if I traveled enough to earn those premier statuses without trying, but it's not worth it to me to fly extra trips just to earn status. They don't mean as much as they used to.

Still, it's worth it to do a few simple things, like those I outlined above, to get basically free trips every year. I still pay for some trips, but I'm able to travel much more because I spend a little time to get the cards and keep the system going.

Chapter 18

My Packing List

I've basically described my packing list in different chapters, but I thought I'd share my list here just to have it in one place.

Of course, this list is just the basic list, but it changes each trip depending on conditions and what my plans are. What I bring almost always looks pretty close to this list, though.

Leo's Packing List

Here's the basic list:
Packing

- Backpack: Minaal Daily

- Cuben fiber toiletry bag

- Eagle Creek packing sacks (one for clothes, smaller one for electronics)

Clothes

- Outlier chinos (pants, worn)

- Workout T-shirt (worn)

My Packing List

- Converse-style shoes (worn)
- Running socks (1 worn, 2 packed)
- Underwear (1 worn, 3 packed)
- Extra T-shirt
- Workout shorts
- Synthetic lightweight long sleeve T-shirt or fleece hoodie
- Patagonia Houdini (ultralight windbreaker/rain jacket)
- Beanie
- Sometimes: long underwear (if it's cold) or heavier jacket/layers

Electronics

- Macbook (ultralight 2016 model)
- Macbook cord
- iPhone
- Cords for Macbook and iPhone
- Mophie power reserve (1,300mAh, 1.5 oz)
- Kikkerland universal adapter

Toiletries

- Travel toothbrush
- Travel toothpaste
- Travel deodorant

- Travel electric clippers (for shaving my head)
- Dental floss
- Ibuprofen (6 pills, just in case)
- Leuko tape (small roll, for blister prevention)
- Nail clippers
- Ear plugs
- Eye mask
- Razor (I use soap to shave my face with this razor)

Other

- Supr Slim Wallet (just a few cards and cash)
- Passport
- Vapur collapsible water bottle
- Maybe some fruit and nut bars

I don't claim this is the perfect packing list, nor that everyone should copy this. But it works for me!

Chapter 19

Ultralight Hiking

As someone who loves hiking and going into the mountains . . . and someone who likes to travel lightly . . . stumbling upon a forum and some blogs and YouTube channels about ultralight backpacking/hiking was quite a discovery.

It was like discovering a goldmine. I ate up the information about people cutting their pack weight down to ridiculously light loads, about shaving weight and finding ultralight solutions . . . it was like heaven to me.

So I did a *lot* of research, got some gear, and started going into the wilderness with very little on my back. I got my base weight (what's in your pack, minus consumables like food and water) down to about 6 lbs., and learned to eat lightweight but calorie-dense foods without cooking (so I didn't need to bring a stove, cooking pot and fuel) so that my total pack weight (including consumables) was down to about 13 lbs.

It felt amazing to hike 20–30 miles with such a light pack! You can go farther and faster and more comfortably with an ultralight backpack.

I'm not saying you should do it, but here are some things I learned:

1. **Cut down on the big three**. The heaviest things in most people's packs are shelter, sleeping stuff (like mattress and sleeping bag) and backpack. You can shave down little things, but cutting down on the big ones will make the most difference. The Thermarest Neoair Xlite mattress is the pad I chose, just 12 oz., and I learned about sleeping quilts (instead of sleeping bags) and tarp shelters or tarp tents to save a ton on shelters. Get the backpack last, once you know how much you have to put in it, but I like the MLD Burn (just 12 oz.) as a good lightweight option.

2. **Cut out the unnecessary**. This will seem obvious if you've read the rest of this book. But lots of people bring things like camp chairs and slippers, knives and all kinds of cooking and eating gear, axes and all kinds of emergency stuff . . . that just isn't needed. It takes some research and experience to learn what you can cut, but there's a lot.

3. **Find high calorie foods**. Most of us want low calorie foods with lots of fiber and water and low sugar and so on . . . but for ultralight hiking, you actually want little water and lots of fat and calories. I go for foods that are around 5 calories per gram (or higher). Actually, I just eat snacks instead of cooking meals. But most people wouldn't like that, so figure out what works for you.

4. **Hike in shorts, trail shoes, long-sleeve shirt, and hat**. When you're hiking, you warm up, so shorts are great. A long-sleeve running shirt works to protect you from the sun, as does a wide-brimmed hat. Trail shoes are light but good for trails, no need for heavy boots (strengthen your ankles by hiking more) or waterproof shoes (they trap in your sweat, your feet will get wet no matter what).

5. **Try to make your items multi-use**. Trekking poles, for example, can also serve as tarp poles. Duct tape can be used for tarp repair or first aid. A puffy jacket can be used as a pillow. If you can use items for multiple things, you can bring less and make the most of what you do bring.

There are tons of other things I've learned, including not packing my fears (I don't bring much in terms of first aid except ibuprofen and leukotape), shaving weight in little ways, etc. Go to reddit.com/r/ultralight for more great info.

This isn't about hitting a certain number, nor showing off how light you've gotten. It's not about sacrificing safety and comfort. In fact, you want to see if you can go light while still being safe and comfortable. Lightweight can make you *more* safe and comfortable. I love it, to be honest.

Part II

LIVING LIGHTLY

In this (shorter) part of the book, I'd like to expand the ideas of traveling light. Let's apply the philosophy to the rest of your life.

What is it like to travel through your ordinary life without the burdens? To live with greater flexibility and freedom? Let's explore!

Chapter 20

What It's like to Live without Too Much Stuff

Imagine a bedroom with a bed and a nightstand, a single drawer for clothes. Just a handful of things hanging in your closet. A few boxes of items stored below those hanging clothes.

The kitchen has mostly bare counters. Cupboards aren't full of stuff, the fridge doesn't need more than a couple shelves of food. Living room is a couch and a shelf with books, no TV.

I'm not saying my life is that minimal, as I have a family with a wife and kids. But if I were alone, or just with a wife, that would basically be my life. With some extra couple boxes in the garage for storage, and some workout equipment.

Even with the wife and kids, that's a good description of my personal items. I like my life that way. Even counting the kids' stuff, we don't have a lot.

What we do have is space. Space to read, write, work, learn, eat, play. We don't have to do a lot of cleaning, because everything pretty much has a place. There isn't a lot of clutter to gather dust. It's easy to clean the counters and table when done using them, and put things where they belong. Declutter every now and then.

What we also have is freedom. Freedom from the burdens of stuff. Not having to dig through a lot of things to find what we're looking for. Easy to put things away because it's clear where they belong.

I'm not saying we're perfect. We have clutter drawers and parts of our garage and closets get cluttered. We do clear them up after awhile, but we're definitely not perfect. And we buy more than we should, ordering on Amazon more than we need to, like most people.

We're not perfect, we have clutter, we buy more than we should. And yet, we live lightly, and I enjoy that kind of life, with space and joy and love.

Chapter 21

Less Clothing

For me, a big part of learning to live lightly was reducing the clothes I needed. I learned that I didn't need a lot of clothes to be comfortable, but I had to let go of some old ideas.

Those old ideas included:

1. That I need to wear something different every day.
2. That I needed to impress people with my clothes.
3. That my identity was tied to how I dressed.
4. That I needed different kinds of clothes for different occasions.

Once I learned that these weren't necessary ideas, it opened up a new world for me. I could wear the same clothes every day, to all kinds of events and meetings. I didn't need a lot of things to impress people or show who I am.

That freed me up to create a very basic wardrobe with just a few plain colors. The purpose of the wardrobe just to be dressed plainly, so that I didn't have to worry about how I'd dress.

My clothes could be cut to something like:

- A few basic T-shirts in solid colors
- One pair of pants
- Two or three workout shorts and shirts
- Some underwear and socks
- Converse-style sneakers
- Running shoes
- A couple long sleeve layers for colder weather, including a fleece hoody and/or puffy jacket

Yes, I could cut that down even more if I wanted, but I like this setup. It's a little more than I travel with, but not much more.

Does it mean I don't have any fun with my clothing? Yes. I decided I don't need clothes to have fun in life. I focus on non-possessions for fun. That means I'm free from worrying about how I dress, free from having too much stuff, free from looking through a whole bunch of clothes to find what I want. It's simple and light.

I don't expect everyone to dress this way, but I thought I'd share some of my ideas in case you're interested in trying it.

Chapter 22

Books and Papers

For a book-lover like me, and for a lot of people, it's hard to let go of books. It's also hard to sort through the stacks of personal documents, bills, and work papers that you might have.

But simplifying these areas is worth it, because it helps us to let go of some of our mental and physical burdens that are in our homes and office spaces.

So here's what I've learned:

1. **Books are hopes**: Books are the hardest things for me to let go of, because each one represents a hope. A hope that I'll read more, that I'll explore this author and this adventure, that I'll learn about this topic, that I'll get through all of these exciting titles!

2. **Limit books**: But if I'm honest, there are only so many books I'm going to read in a month, in a year. There's no way I'm going to read all those books. And if I've already read them, for the most part I'm not going to read them again, they're just trophies. So I've learned to let go of books that I have hopes for, but that are realistically never going to be read. Let's say I think I can read 2 books a month (optimistic) . . . that's 24 books

in a year. The rest I can gift to people, give to charity, or sell.

3. **Digital books**: I actually like reading both paper books and on the Kindle. If I get books on the Kindle, I don't need all the paper books. So I get rid of most of those, even if I love them. This is a letting go process that's good for me.

4. **Scan papers**: Papers can be scanned and put into online storage like Dropbox. Very few papers need to be kept in hardcopy format anymore—even copies of tax returns can be digital. I keep some documents like marriage and birth certificates in a folder, but even those have digital copies. I have a handful of folders in Dropbox (taxes, leases, bills, other important documents, some work stuff) and scan everything into these folders. They're backed up, available online from anywhere, and take up very little space on my computer (much less than music or photos, for example).

5. **Chunks**: It can be overwhelming to have to scan in stacks and stacks of papers. So you can just do it a little at a time, for 5–10 minutes a day, and eventually you'll be done. Or get someone else to do it—I paid my teen-age kids to do it, and there are services that will do it for you as well.

So that's the basic system. Only keep as many books as you can realistically read in a year (6 months is even better), read mostly on Kindle anyway, scan all your papers and put them in Dropbox folders (or another similar service).

With this kind of system, you have very few hard copies of documents, you don't require lots of book shelf space, and things are simple and easy.

Chapter 23

Less Other Stuff

In the last two chapters, I covered clothes, books and papers . . . but what about all the other things in your life? There can be so many that I'm not going to write a chapter about all of them.

What I'll do is cover them here briefly, room by room.

Living Room

If you have a living room, it might be full of furniture and other stuff. Why not cut it down to a minimum? That makes the space less cluttered, and more pleasant to spend time in. For example:

- A couch and a chair or love seat, for lounging
- A table for putting books and tea
- A shelf or cabinet for books and other items
- A desk for a computer, if you work here
- A meditation cushion

That's mostly what you'd need, and you could cut back on a couple of these, depending on what you like to do. And of course, you could add a TV and/or entertainment center. We use a projector to watch movies or TV shows, but we don't have a TV set.

What's missing is all the little things you'll often find cluttering up people's living rooms. Clear those out!

Kitchen

With a large family that likes to cook at home, we have more stuff in our kitchen than a lot of true minimalists. That said, we don't keep our kitchen counters cluttered. Here's how:

- Keep single-use appliances, like toasters and waffle makers, to a minimum. To be honest, this has grown for us over the last five years. We could cut this down even further.

- Not too many dishes. Enough for our family and some guests..

- Not too many pots and pans. Cut to a minimum, and then only add over time if needed.

- A basic pantry for cooking, but not full of snacks or other prepared foods.

- Keep the counters as clear as possible. Our counters have a coffeemaker and grinder, olive oil near the stove, a kettle for hot water, and a cup for each of us that we reuse for water throughout the day.

If you don't have a lot of kids, I would suggest you need fewer dishes and fewer pots and pans than us. Mainly, keep the counters clear and clean!

Bedroom

For me, the bedroom is for sleeping, reading and dressing. Sometimes Eva uses it for sewing. But that's about it. So that means we have just:

- One bed and a couple of nightstands (for reading and sleeping stuff like a backlight and eye mask).
- A dresser (one drawer for me, a few more for her).
- A table for sewing.
- A closet with clothing and sheets and some travel stuff stored in there. A handful of other things as well.
- Nothing on the floors but the furniture mentioned above. Nothing on top of the dresser or night stands. Keep things uncluttered!

Bathroom

For me, I don't need a lot of things in the bathroom for grooming, other than stuff to shave my face and hair, nail clippers, soap for showering, and some cotton swabs.

Of course, Eva has a few more things than me. But we try to keep the counter area near the sink fairly clear (just a couple things for each of us on the counter). Nothing on the floor but bathroom rugs and a bathroom trash can.

Garage/Storage

Stuff that you need to store tends to build up over time. I suggest a regular clearing out. Hold a garage sale once a year, or donate stuff to charity.

For us, the things that are in our garage include:

- Workout stuff (see below)
- Christmas decorations
- Bikes
- Camping and sports equipment (balls, tents, etc.)
- A couple boxes of miscellaneous things

Not the most minimal, but not a crazy amount for a family of our size. We also have a couple storage closets. One closet is for coats and shoes and umbrellas. Another closet seems to have become a temporary storage space for stuff we're getting rid of. We also keep some big futons in this closet that we got for when we had lots of family visiting and not enough beds.

The idea is to try to stop the buildup of storage items by reducing it to a minimum on a regular basis. Don't just throw things in there—keep it organized. And if it's not, slowly reduce and organize into storage containers/boxes.

Exercise/Outdoor Activities

I think it's worth having possessions that encourage you and your family to get active, workout, go outside. So we have:

- A full weight set in the garage (squat rack, bench, barbell, plates, dumbbells)—practically our entire family uses this now, not just me anymore. Totally worth it for us.
- A rowing machine—to be honest, this was a hope-filled purchase, and while we have used it, not enough to justify the purchase.

Less Other Stuff 79

- Camping equipment in some big plastic storage bins (tents, sleeping bags and pads, some camp cooking stuff, etc.).
- Bikes and some bike equipment (pump, helmets, headlights, locks).
- Sports stuff—mostly different kinds of balls.

This is more than I'd have if I were living alone. But I like to encourage our kids (and me and Eva) to get outside and get active, so we've invested in all this stuff. That means our garage is mostly a "Get Active" center, not storage and not for our car (which parks outside).

Chapter 24

Electronics and Digital Simplicity

Applying the ideas of living lightly to our digital lives is an interesting exercise. Our lives have increasingly become about our devices and the digital space inside them, which is not necessarily a bad thing. It just changes the dynamics.

On the one hand, a couple of devices (a laptop and phone, for example), might replace a lot of the physical stuff we used to own:

- Paper books—read on the phone.

- Albums, VHS, DVDs and CDs—watch and listen on devices.

- TVs, stereos, typewriters, GPS devices, fax machines, printers—replace with these devices.

- File cabinets, documents and folders—replace with digital files and communications.

- Physical photo albums—increasingly rare, usually digital these days.

Electronics and Digital Simplicity

- Maps, globes, scrapbooks, journals, notebooks, sketchpads and more—replace with digital stuff.
- Cameras, camcorders, film and film canisters, DVD players, VHS players, and more—now just a phone.

There are just a few examples of how our devices can save physical clutter by being the multipurpose machines we never imagined just 20 years ago.

But another kind of clutter has emerged—digital and device clutter.

Device Clutter

These days, it's easy to have a lot of devices:

- Desktop computer
- Laptop
- Phone
- Tablet
- iPod
- Smart watch
- Kindle
- Amazon Echo
- Streaming device (Apple TV, Roku, Chromecast, etc.)
- TV
- Stereo
- Portable router and/or wifi
- Digital camera and/or GoPro video camera

- All the cables and chargers that go with these
- And more

It's possible to narrow these down, just like in the other areas of our lives. Everyone's needs are different, so I won't presume to tell you what to use. However, here's one possible setup:

1. Phone (skip the iPod, Kindle, and tablet)
2. Laptop (skip the desktop computer)
3. Streaming device for TV watching, with a home theater projector and speakers

So you'd skip the digital camera, Echo, smart watch, TV, stereo. Anyway, this is *mostly* what I have, except I also use a desktop computer for video editing. I could do without the desktop without much trouble. Again, your needs will vary.

Digital Clutter

What devices you have matter less than simplifying what you do on them. You can often reduce what you do on your devices and how you organize everything.

A "one thing at a time" approach is a great place to start. Focus on one thing instead of constantly switching between tabs and applications. Some examples:

- Focus on important tasks and close everything else. Don't let yourself switch to other tasks for at least 10 minutes.
- Bookmark all tabs and put them into "read later" app or on your todo list. Then close the tabs, so you can focus on one task.

- When you read, use a "read later" service like Instapaper. Close everything else. Read one article/blog post at a time.
- When you process email, do one at a time. Read it, then take one of the following actions: 1) reply and archive, 2) delete or archive it, 3) forward and archive, 4) put it on your to-do list and star/flag and archive it (so you'll have it in a "starred" folder for action. If you work your way through the inbox like this, you'll get everything out of your inbox.

To keep things organized, I have a set of "buckets" that I keep everything in:

- **Files**: I put these in a set of Dropbox folders so they're always synced and backed up. Folders for finances, important documents, work projects, personal memories, etc. I keep everything in places I can easily find them later, and don't have to worry about them again.
- **Photos**: I like to have them all backed up online. There are lots of ways to do that: Google Photos, Apple's iCloud, Dropbox, or your own server (for privacy).
- **Saved websites**: I like to save web pages I want to remember for future reference, so I put them in Pinboard.in. It's not free, though, so you could just save them in your browser's bookmarks folder. As long as you have a place you can go to for them later.
- **Read later articles**: I use Instapaper, though there are lots of others: Safari's Read Later list, Pocket, and more. The idea is to have one place where you put things you want to read, so you can go there when you have spare reading time.
- **Action items**: Add all action items to a todo list. Lately I've been using Todoist, but I've used many good todo

apps, and have also just used paper and pen or a plain text file. The key is to have them all in one place, including actions from emails and browser tabs that you need to remember.

- **Calendar events**: If it's something you have to do on a specific day or time, put them in your go-to calendar.

- **Travel info**: I put all trip information into Tripit. But if you use Google Docs or some other app or folder, that's fine too.

- **Finances**: I use Mint.com to import all my banking and credit card data, so I can see my finances in one place. I check this daily, actually, so I always know how things are going.

There are probably a few other buckets I've forgotten to mention, but these are my main ones. This system means you always know where your digital information is, and it's not hard to maintain.

Chapter 25

Dealing with the Urge to Buy

Reducing your stuff down to a minimalist setup is one thing, but it means little if you quickly build it up again by buying more stuff. And what I've discovered is that you can't avoid the buildup of stuff over time. We naturally acquire things. We get gifts, take home free stuff from events, and generally get more and more without reducing.

So there are a few things I recommend as rules to help with this tendency. But even more important for the long term is learning mindfully to deal with the urges to buy things. We'll talk about that in a minute, but first, my suggested rules:

Here are the rules:

- **A 30-day waiting list**. Put it on a 30-day list with the date you added it to the list. Don't let yourself buy anything until it's been on the list for 30 days. This obviously doesn't apply to groceries or other necessities like toiletries and medicine. This rule keeps you from buying things on impulse.

- **Don't get stuff for new hobbies**. I'm most guilty in this area. I get into a new hobby, like hiking or chess, and then get a bunch of equipment or books. And this is fine, until I move on to the next hobby and start all over again. I leave the old hobby equipment and books to gather dust for a year until I get interested again. So my new rule is to not get stuff for new hobbies. Or at least wait a month before ordering anything.

- **Don't take free stuff**. If you run a 5K or go to a conference, they'll give you free stuff to take home. Yay! But that's rarely anything you really need, and it just ends up cluttering your life. Instead, just say no to the free stuff.

- **Talk to people about not giving you gifts**. Similarly, gifts are wonderful expressions of someone's love for you, but they end up adding to your built-up clutter. Instead, talk to the loved ones in your life about spending time together instead of giving each other new possessions. Perhaps go on a hike or picnic together instead of giving a new sweater. Make something consumable: give each other baked goods, make a dinner for the other person.

- **Think mindfully about what you bring into your life**. This is a general rule that applies to all the things above. Think carefully about whether you really need this item. Where will it go in your home, how much care it will take, whether it will add joy to your life or serve your life's purpose. Is it worth adding to your life?

- **Declutter at regular intervals**. Even if you do all of the above, things will still start to build up in your life. Once you've decluttered, you just need to revisit areas in your home and office at regular intervals. I've found that every six months is a good interval. Put it on your calendar, and for about a week pick an area and do a sweep of what's in it and what you don't need anymore.

Dealing Mindfully with Urges

To be honest, I give in to the urge to buy stuff, just like anyone else. I'm not immune to consumerist urges, and so I'm not going to act holier than thou.

However, I do find it useful to be mindful of the urges, and to work with them. When I do, I buy less and regret my purchases less. :)

So here's how to work with urges to purchase stuff:

1. **Notice the urge.** Learn to notice when you have the urge to buy something. Good hints that you have the urge to buy something include going to your favorite shopping site or wanting to rush off to a store.

2. **Sit with the urge.** Instead of running off and acting on the urge, or trying to distract yourself from it . . . try facing it. Sit still and watch the urge build up in you, see how it feels physically in your body. Notice the energy in your body. Stay with it, watching it, not acting but observing.

3. **See the story.** It's interesting to notice what "story" you're telling yourself that's causing this urge. A story might be something like: "These new shoes will make me feel cool (or sexy)." Or "I'll be active and fit if I buy this kayak (or Apple Watch, etc.)". These stories seem very real, but the truth is they're just movies playing in our heads. The movies cause us to want something or feel a certain way. We can notice the stories and not let them control us. We can realize that they're not completely real but more like a dream.

4. **Find appreciation for the present moment.** Drop out of the story, and instead notice the moment in front of you. See the light, notice sounds, feel the

physical sensations. And find appreciation for the wonder that's in front of you right now. It's amazing, and it's free. And you don't need to buy anything to find contentment and joy right now.

Chapter 26

A Final Word on Living Lightly

At home, you don't carry everything on your back, as you do when you travel. So the need to reduce your load isn't felt as strongly. You can get away with some extra weight stuffed into a closet.

But I've found that it does matter. You don't have to have the perfect home—I know I'm far from perfect. But living lightly does make a difference.

When you live lightly, you create space for living, without all the clutter. You free your mind from having to worry about all the stuff in your life. Your life isn't so full of stuff that you have to tread carefully between piles of clutter. You don't have to push stuff aside so that you can get things done. Nor rummage through stuff to find what you're looking for. These are small things, but they add up through the course of a day, the course of a lifetime.

You should live your life as you like, not as I prescribe. I've just found a lot of joy in lightening my load, and I hope some of these ideas give you inspiration to find your own joy in letting go of what you previously thought you couldn't.

About the Author

Leo Babauta is the creator of Zen Habits, and author of the *Zen Habits* book as well as *Essential Zen Habits*. He has helped thousands of people change their habits, simplify their lives and practice mindfulness through his blog and his Sea Change membership program. He lives in Davis, California with his wife and six kids (several of whom are now adults!). He's a vegan, and enjoys running, reading, meditating, lifting weights and hiking.

www.ingramcontent.com/pod-product-compliance
Lightning Source LLC
Chambersburg PA
CBHW071621040426
42452CB00009B/1435